MW00345402

Sweet Tarts for my Sweethearts

Stories & Recipes from a Culinary Career

Bonnie Lee Black

Sweet Tarts for My Sweethearts:
Stories & Recipes from a Culinary Career

Copyright © 2020, Bonnie Lee Black

www.bonnieleeblack.com

All rights reserved.

No part of this publication may be reproduced, stored in a retrieval system, or transmitted, in any form or by any means, electronic, mechanical, photocopying, recording, or otherwise, without the prior written permission of the author.

Cover and interior design: Kathleen Munroe, www.starrdesign.biz

Cover photo: Kharin Gilbert

Dedication page photo: Thomas X. Loughlin

Interior photos: Kharin Gilbert and Bonnie Lee Black

Type is set in Calluna and Apple Chancery

ISBN 978-1-7334483-3-8

Published by Nighthawk Press, Taos, New Mexico
Printed in the United States of America

Other books by Bonnie Lee Black:
Somewhere Child, Viking Press, New York, 1981
How to Cook a Crocodile, Peace Corps Writers, 2010
How to Make an African Quilt, Nighthawk Press, 2013
Jamie's Muse (a novel), Nighthawk Press, 2018

For Claire & Charlotte, my littlest sweethearts

Contents

*O*f all the things I've loved to cook and to bake over the years, making sweet tarts for loved ones and special occasions has topped the list. This cookbook is a compilation of some of my favorite, tried-and-true sweet tart recipes, along with related stories, drawn from my twenty-year culinary career. I hope that Sweet Tarts *will inspire you to make one or two — or more — of these recipes from time to time, especially on special occasions, and enjoy them with your own sweethearts.*

Bonnie Lee Black
San Miguel de Allende, Mexico
September 2020

A Sweet Tarts Story

Once upon a time, a long time ago now, I fantasized about opening a small, French-style patisserie on the Upper West Side of Manhattan, near where I lived, specializing in dessert tarts.

I could see it all so clearly in my mind: The shop on the ground floor of an old brownstone building on a side street off of upper Broadway; the name out front in charming lettering, "Sweet Tarts"; the tinkling bell over the front door announcing customers' entrances; the gleaming glass display cases showing off my proud handiwork, such as apple, raspberry, pear, plum, pecan, and lemon tarts and tartlets.

Yes, I would make all the dazzling, jewel-like tarts by hand by myself. Of course, the ingredients would be the freshest and best quality. And my secret ingredient, *bien sûr*, would be love.

The New York Times would do a write-up on my "Sweet Tarts" shop, and customers would arrive in droves (*quelle fantasie!*). I would be tired, but not as tired as I'd become from catering in New York for ten years. This new venture would be small, specialized, steady, and close to home. I'd be doing what I loved most to do: baking beautiful, regal, crown-like tarts and making people happy in the process.

Ah, but there's nothing like cold, hard, sharp numbers to pierce a dream balloon. To do what I dreamed of doing in Manhattan would have taken serious money, which I didn't have. Nor did I have friends or friends of friends with deep pockets willing to back such a venture. (Well, I didn't have the nerve to ask around.) The idea never went beyond a sweet fantasy.

Instead, at the age of fifty-one, I closed my ten-year-old catering business and joined the Peace Corps, ready for a big change. I served as a health and nutrition volunteer in the rainforest of Gabon, Central Africa, for two years, during which time I taught simple cooking techniques. I never had occasion to bake a dessert tart nor even see or eat one. In the interior of Africa there are few such frills. Butter is a rarity, and the flour is speckled with bugs.

I never returned to New York City to live. New York, I knew too well by then, is a city for young dreamers who have the wherewithal to make those dreams happen. It was time for me to move on. But the sweet pastry shop "Sweet Tarts" still, to this day, exists in my mind and in my heart.

Mom's Apple Pie

My mother, Lee Black, was the best pie baker in the world.
Well, at least in *my* world. As her eldest daughter and acolyte,
I stood beside her at our kitchen table in Hillsdale, New Jersey, as a
child in the early fifties and watched in awe her pie-making magic.
Her cool, slender, manicured hands worked quickly and deftly. She
knew what she was doing.

"You must work fast," she told me softly, without looking up
from the flour-strewn table. It was just the two of us in that tiny
kitchen. My older brother was out playing baseball with his buddies,
and my younger sisters were upstairs napping. This was my time to
have my mother all to myself, and I savored it. "Pie dough mustn't be
over-handled or it will be tough like cardboard," she said. "Nobody
likes cardboard pies."

Of course, her pie pastry was always light and flaky, just as it
was supposed to be. She credited her success to her experience and
technique, as well as to Crisco.

I watched her cut the pure white blobs of Crisco into the bowl of
flour with a hand-held pastry blender, then dribble in just the right
amount of ice water, then form the crumbly mass into a smooth ball.
I watched her roll the dough on the floured table with her ancient,
rickety, wooden rolling pin, running her left hand over the surface of
the dough from time to time, to check for even thickness. I watched

as she folded the rolled-out dough over her rolling pin and airlifted it onto her favorite nine-inch Pyrex pie dish. I watched as she trimmed the overhang with a knife, reinforced the rim with thin strips of dough gently glued on with pats of cold water, then crimped the rim with her delicate fingers before pouring in the filling, such as soupy pumpkin custard redolent with Autumn spices.

She accomplished all this at what seemed to me to be lightning speed, and I worried even as I stood at her side that I'd never in a million years be able to follow her lead. It was well known in my family that my top speed for accomplishing anything was Slow. In fact, my mother's affectionate nickname for me was Molasses. But I watched silently, taking careful mental notes, all the while knowing I'd likely never become the pie-maker that she was.

I have vivid pictures in my mind of some of her pies — towering, ethereal Lemon Meringue, its snowy peaks tinged with caramelized streaks; mountainous, golden, double-crusted Apple, with slits in the top, allowing the cinnamon-scented steam to escape; coppery, shimmering Pumpkin that became for me the full, harvest-moon-face of Thanksgiving — all with the pretty, frilly raised edges she was so proud of. Her pies would surely have won prizes in state fairs, if she'd ever thought to enter them.

She experimented with new pies occasionally, too, because her little kitchen was her laboratory, and when it came to cooking she was always on a quest. She read her favorite magazines, *Woman's Day* and *Good Housekeeping*, with scissors in her right hand, clipping new recipes that intrigued her. Along the way, she discovered a new, for her, way to bake an apple pie — enclosed in a brown paper bag in the oven. Paper Bag Apple Pie, then, became her personal favorite, so much so that one of my sisters later painted the recipe decoratively

on a wooden plaque that proudly hung on the wall of my mother's
kitchen for decades.

Lee's Paper Bag Apple Pie

Prepare an unbaked 9-inch pastry shell

Peel, core, and quarter four large baking apples,
then cut each quarter in half, crosswise, to make chunks.

Drizzle apple chunks with 2 tablespoons of freshly squeezed lemon juice.

Combine ½ cup sugar, 2 tablespoons flour, ½ teaspoon nutmeg
(or cinnamon); sprinkle this mixture over apples and toss.

Spoon apples into pastry shell.

For the topping:

Combine ½ cup sugar, ½ cup flour, and ½ cup (1 stick) butter;
sprinkle this mixture over apples to cover top.

Slide pie into large brown paper bag; secure open end tightly;
place on a large cookie sheet.

Bake at 425 degrees for 1 hour.

Remove from bag and cool on a wire rack.

While it's true I've never managed to become the pie-maker
that Lee was, I've taken the liberty of adapting her favorite apple pie
recipe into a tart. I'm sure if she were alive today she would like it
and approve.

Mom's Oven Bag Apple Tart

For Pastry

*Prepare 1 partially baked 9" tart shell.**

Ingredients

- 4 baking apples (such as Granny Smith or Golden Delicious — or a combination), peeled, cored, quartered, sliced, and cut into dime-size chunks
- 2 tablespoons freshly squeezed lemon juice
- 1 cup sugar, divided
- ½ cup, plus 2 tablespoons flour
- ½ teaspoon ground cinnamon or freshly grated nutmeg
- 1 stick (½ cup) cold, unsalted butter, cut into chunks
- (Optional: ¼ cup finely chopped slivered almonds)

Procedure

1. Preheat oven to 400 degrees. In a large bowl, toss apple chunks with lemon juice.

2. In another bowl, combine ½ cup sugar, 2 tablespoons flour, and cinnamon or nutmeg. Sprinkle this mixture over apples and toss. Spoon into tart shell.

3. Make topping: Combine remaining ½ cup sugar, ½ cup flour, butter chunks and (optional) chopped almonds in a bowl and pinch with your fingertips until crumbly; sprinkle this crumbly mixture over apples to cover top.

4. Slide tart into a "turkey size" Reynolds Oven Bag — carefully following the directions on the box; secure open end, and place on a baking sheet.

5. Bake at 400 degrees for about one hour, until top is golden and bubbly. Remove from bag and cool on a wire rack.

---

* If tart pastry making is new for you, please be sure to read the Pastry chapter beginning on page 67 for all of your options and the step-by-step directions.

An Apple Tart Tour of France

*T*arts are to France what pies are to the U.S.A. And just as apple is the quintessential American pie, apple tarts feature proudly in all of the major apple-growing regions of France.

When I lived in New York for twenty years and Paris was just an arm's reach across the Atlantic, I visited my favorite European city as frequently as possible, staying with my French friend Marie-Laure Besançon in her apartment in the 16th Arrondissement. Especially after I became a food professional in Manhattan in the mid-eighties, Paris became for me Culinary Mecca, and my visits took on a religious fervor. Only the French, I thought then (and still do) could make desserts — above all, their jewel-like, open-faced fruit tarts — that make one want to fall to her knees in adoration, light a votive candle, and recite a prayer of thanks.

In Paris's patisseries I especially ogled the glisteningly glazed, flower-patterned apple tarts framed by frilly golden pastry, aching to be taken home in a wicker market basket. Outside of Paris, in the lush countryside, I saw that farm wives dispense with the frilly tart pan all together and make free-form apple tarts, or galettes, as their grandmothers and great-grandmothers did before them.

Normandy, to the north, one of France's greatest gastronomic regions, is a land not only of milk and honey but also of cream, eggs, butter, apples and cider, which are the foundations of the region's cooking and baking. As in Normandy, the apple tarts made in France's eastern Alsace region are often enriched with creamy-eggy custard.

An all together different type of apple tart, one that originated in the central region of France, is the celebrated Tarte Tatin. What began as a flop, it is said, in an inn in Sologne, when one of the Tatin proprietresses dropped her freshly made apple tart upside down, has since become one of the classic recipes of France and ubiquitous around the world.

When I had my catering business, Bonnie Fare Catering, in New York, I would sometimes bake individual Tarte Tatins in blini pans for sit-down dinner parties, serve them warm with a dollop of sweetened, vanilla-flavored whipped cream, and listen from the kitchen for the guests' *ooohs* and *ahhhhhs*. Later, I baked my Tarte Tatins in a 9-inch diameter cast iron Le Creuset sauté pan and served them in generous slices.

Here are my favorite versions of some of France's most renowned apple tarts.

Parisian Apple Tart

For Pastry

Prepare 1 partially baked 9" tart shell.*

Ingredients

- 4 medium-size cooking apples (such as Golden Delicious) peeled, cored and thinly sliced
- ½ cup sugar
- 4 tablespoons (½ stick) cold unsalted butter, cut into small dice
- ½ cup apricot or apple jelly
- 2 tablespoons rum (or water)

Procedure

1. Preheat oven to 400 degrees. Arrange the apple slices on the tart shell in a rose pattern, covering the pastry with the apple slices. Sprinkle with sugar and dot with the diced butter.

2. Bake for 30 to 45 minutes, until the pastry is browned and the edges of the apples start to brown.

3. When the tart is done, heat the jelly with the rum (or water) and brush the apples and the pastry completely with the jelly mixture. Allow tart to cool slightly before serving warm or at room temperature.

----

* If tart pastry making is new for you, please be sure to read the Pastry chapter beginning on page 67 for all of your options and the step-by-step directions.

French Farm-Style Apple Galette

For Pastry

Prepare 1 galette pastry (page 71).

Ingredients

- 6 medium Gala (or Granny Smith) apples
- ⅓ cup, plus 2 tablespoons apple jelly
- 1 tablespoon freshly squeezed lemon juice
- ¼ cup granulated sugar
- 1 tablespoon flour (such as Wondra, if available)
- Egg wash (made from one egg yolk whisked with 1 tablespoon water)
- 1 tablespoon unsalted butter, cut into small dice

Procedure

1. Make applesauce: Peel, core, and finely chop two of the apples and combine with ⅓ cup apple jelly plus 2 tablespoons of water in a microwave-safe glass bowl. Cover and microwave on High for about 8 minutes, stopping to stir from time to time, until apples are soft. (Can also, of course, be made in a saucepan on the stovetop.) Mash to applesauce consistency. Set aside. (Can be made ahead, covered, and refrigerated for several days.)

2. Preheat oven to 425 degrees. Roll dough into a 13" round and transfer to a parchment-lined baking sheet. Sprinkle flour over center of dough, leaving a 2" border all around. Spread the applesauce over this flour.

3. Peel, core, and quarter remaining four apples, cutting each quarter into three slices. Toss apple slices in a bowl with lemon juice, then mound apples on top of the applesauce; sprinkle with sugar.

4. Fold dough border over apples, pleating gently. Use egg wash as "glue" between pleats and as gloss over surface of pastry. Bake about 40 minutes, or until golden.

5. Melt the remaining 2 tablespoons of apple jelly with 1 teaspoon water in a small saucepan. Use this glaze to brush over the tops of the apples when the galette comes out of the oven.

If tart pastry making is new for you, please be sure to read the Pastry chapter beginning on page 67 for all of your options and the step-by-step directions.

Norman Apple Tart

For Pastry

Prepare 1 prebaked 9" or 10" tart shell. *

Ingredients

- 3 medium-size cooking apples, such as Russet or Golden Delicious, quartered, cored, peeled, and each quarter cut into four equal slices
- ¼ cup Calvados (apple brandy)
- ¼ cup plus 2 tablespoons sugar
- 3 egg yolks
- 1 cup heavy cream
- ¼ cup finely slivered almonds

Procedure

1. In a medium-size bowl, gently toss the apple slices in the Calvados; cover with plastic wrap and allow apples to soak in the Calvados for one hour.

2. Preheat the oven to 350 degrees. Sprinkle the 2 tablespoons of sugar over the prebaked tart shell. Drain apple slices, reserving the Calvados, and place the slices on top of the sugar in a flower design. Bake at 350 degrees for 30 min.

3. Increase oven heat to 425. Beat egg yolks, cream, remaining ¼ cup sugar and reserved Calvados and pour this over the apples. Scatter the almonds on top and bake for an additional 15-20 minutes, until custard is firm and top is golden.

---

* *If tart pastry making is new for you, please be sure to read the Pastry chapter beginning on page 67 for all of your options and the step-by-step directions.*

Alsatian Apple Tart

For Pastry

Prepare 1 partially baked 10" tart shell.*

Ingredients

- 3 Golden Delicious apples, quartered, cored, peeled; each quarter cut into four slices
- 4 egg yolks
- ⅓ cup sugar
- ¼ teaspoon vanilla
- ¼ teaspoon cinnamon
- ¾ cup heavy cream

Procedure

1. Preheat oven to 400 degrees. Arrange apple slices in one layer in rose design on pastry shell and bake for 15-20 minutes.

2. Meanwhile, combine the egg yolks, sugar, vanilla, cinnamon, and heavy cream in a bowl and whisk until smooth. Pour custard mixture over apples and bake an additional 35-or-so minutes until custard is set and apples are golden.

---

* *If tart pastry making is new for you, please be sure to read the Pastry chapter beginning on page 67 for all of your options and the step-by-step directions.*

Bonnie Fare Tarte Tatin

For Pastry

1 sheet store-bought puff pastry (such as Pepperidge Farm brand; follow directions on the box for thawing and unfolding)

Ingredients

- ¾ cup sugar
- 3 tablespoons water
- 2 teaspoons freshly squeezed lemon juice
- 4 tablespoons (½ stick) unsalted butter, cut up
- 8-10 Macintosh (or Golden Delicious) apples, peeled, cored, and cut into eighths

Procedure

1. Cut a round from the puff pastry approximately one inch larger than the circumference of the ovenproof sauté pan you've chosen. (I have used a 9″ cast iron Le Creuset sauté pan.) Dock the round of pastry with a fork and keep refrigerated.

2. To make the caramel: Place the sugar, water, and lemon juice in a large, clear, microwavable bowl; cover and microwave

on High about 6-8 minutes, just until amber-colored (watch closely; it overcooks quickly); add butter carefully (to avoid splattering and burning yourself) and stir.

(Caramel can be cooked on the stovetop, of course; however, it's easier to watch and control in a microwave oven.)

3. Preheat oven to 375 degrees. Pour caramel into bottom of your ovenproof sauté pan, add apples,  round side down, decoratively, mounding the pan slightly; and par-cook about 15 minutes on top of the stove, until apples begin to soften and caramelize. Top with round of docked puff pastry, and tuck pastry in on all sides.

4. Place sauté pan on a foil-lined sheet pan (to catch drips) and bake about 25-30 minutes, until golden brown and bubbly. Cool to lukewarm before carefully reversing onto a serving plate.

---

* If tart pastry making is new for you, please be sure to read the Pastry chapter (page 67).

A True Blueberry Story

Second only to my mother in my early culinary influences was Emmy, the cook at the house in Maine where I spent the summer of 1961, the year I turned 16. This was the summer estate in Rockport owned by a wealthy elderly couple from Philadelphia with a staff of faithful old servants, of whom my 73-year-old maternal grandmother was one.

I'd been invited to spend that summer helping my grandmother with her housekeeping chores. ("Close the drain — dry the sink — don't let water marks remain; dust each rung along the stairs — lift each plant — move each chair — " Grandma's instructions to me became a litany I sang to myself that summer.) When those chores were finished, I was free to explore. One of my favorite destinations for exploration was Emmy's cavernous basement kitchen.

Emmy was a large, imposing German woman who clearly preferred to work alone. My grandmother called her "cold" and "unfriendly," but over time Emmy and I managed to become friends. At first, I just watched her silently, the way I'd watched my mother cook when I was a child — without interfering or breaking her concentration, simply taking it all in, like an observant ghost. But little by little Emmy acknowledged me and began to teach me, not just about cooking but also about life.

She had been a pretty young woman — "a lot like you," she said to me, pointing a puffy forefinger at my face — in Germany before "that awful war." After the war began she'd had to run from the bombs. There was no real food. One of her sisters hung herself in their family's home. Her first-and-only-true-love joined the army and died in battle. She grew bone-thin and turned prematurely gray. She could never have children.

I stared, wide-eyed, at her sad, tired face.

"But vee must go on!" she said triumphantly, snapping to attention and slapping with her large, workmanlike hands the roast she was preparing to put into the kitchen's ancient oven. "Vee must live! Vee must eat! Vee must cook good food!" She forced a gap-toothed smile.

One day she gave me a small bucket and urged me to explore farther afield. "Go find blueberries for me," she ordered. "Vild blueberries are so delicious!"

So I spent that afternoon hiking the nearby hills, hunting for blueberry bushes, and filling the bucket for Emmy. When I returned, she and I baked blueberry muffins, not a pie or a tart. But whenever I think of blueberries, and especially when I bake with them, regardless of what I'm making, I always think of Emmy.

BB's Blueberry Tart

For Pastry

Prepare 1 prebaked 8″ tart shell.*

Ingredients

- 3 cups fresh blueberries, washed, picked over, and patted dry
- ¼ cup sugar
- 1 tablespoon quick-cooking tapioca
- 1 tablespoon freshly squeezed lemon juice
- 1 tablespoon mixed berry jam or Framboise liqueur

Procedure

1. Combine 1 cup of the fresh blueberries with the sugar, tapioca, lemon juice and jam or liqueur in a 2-quart Pyrex bowl and microwave on High for 5 minutes. (Can also be made in a saucepan on the stovetop.)

2. Add one cup of the remaining uncooked berries to the above mixture while it is hot; stir well and allow to cool, uncovered.

3. When cool, pour the mixture into the baked tart shell, smoothing the top. Dot the surface with the remaining 1 cup of uncooked blueberries. Dust tart with confectioners' sugar.

---

* *If tart pastry making is new for you, please be sure to read the Pastry chapter beginning on page 67 for all of your options and the step-by-step directions.*

A Catering Love Story

The logo for my catering company, Bonnie Fare Catering, which specialized in at-home dinners and cocktail parties in Manhattan, was a place setting with a red-tartan heart in the center of a dinner plate. The tagline read, "Bonnie Fare means good food." What the logo's design clearly hoped to convey was that I put my heart into my cooking. Because I did.

And being a somewhat romantic, single, youngish woman at the time, in a city not known for its heart, I confess I went a little overboard with the heart theme, like a devout missionary intent on spreading the gospel of love. My movie-star-handsome, smiling waiters served hors d'oeuvres on a heart-shape copper tray. I made individual coeurs a la crème desserts in traditional heart-shape molds, served in a pool of red raspberry sauce. I baked small, heart-shape, sugarcoated Scottish shortbread cookies to accompany after-dinner coffee.

Of course, when Valentine's Day, my favorite holiday of the year, rolled around, I'd go all out. I might, for example, make individual raspberry-studded tartlets in heart shapes, as shown below. Or I might make a simpler variation in a round, 9" tart shell to be shared with special friends.

How To Make
Heart Shaped Tartlets

Procedure

1. Roll 1 sheet of purchased puff pastry (following directions on the box for defrosting and unfolding) on a floured board to about 12 inches square.

2. Cut 8 large heart shapes from the sheet (using a 4-inch wide cookie cutter, or a heart-shape cardboard pattern as your guide).

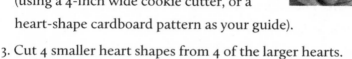

3. Cut 4 smaller heart shapes from 4 of the larger hearts.

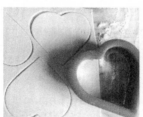

4. Glue the heart-shape strips onto the remaining 4 large hearts with egg wash (1 egg yolk whisked with 1 tablespoon water); dock the centers of these 4 with a fork.

5. With a pastry brush, gently egg wash all 8 of the hearts (that is, the four larger ones and four smaller ones). Bake on a parchment-lined cookie sheet in a preheated 400-degree oven for about 15 minutes, until golden brown. Cool on a wire rack.

6. With a fork, carefully hollow the centers of the larger heart shells, being sure not to pierce the bottom or sides, and discard this excess pastry.

7. Microwave ¾ cup of white chocolate chips until melted, about 2 minutes; whisk until smooth. Spoon melted chocolate into the bottoms and up the insides of the four tart shells. Fill shells with fresh raspberries (about 8-10 raspberries in each).

8. Whip about a ½ cup of heavy cream to soft peaks; add about 1 tablespoon confectioners' sugar and a dash of vanilla and whip to stiffer peaks. Dollop tops of tarts with whipped cream and top each with the smaller puff pastry heart.

9. Dust with confectioners' sugar, if desired.

Raspberry & White Chocolate Valentine Tart

For Pastry

Prepare 1 prebaked 9" tart shell. *

Ingredients

- 1 cup white chocolate chips
- ⅔ cup sweetened condensed milk
- 1 teaspoon vanilla
- 1 pint fresh raspberries
- Confectioners' sugar

Procedure

1. Microwave white chocolate chips with condensed milk until chocolate is melted, about 2–3 minutes. Add vanilla. Stir well.

2. Pour mixture into pastry shell and smooth out. Cover surface with fresh raspberries. Dust with confectioners' sugar.

---

* If tart pastry making is new for you, please be sure to read the Pastry chapter beginning on page 67 for all of your options and the step-by-step directions.

A Matter of Balance

I don't remember where I first discovered this recipe, but I've long since brazenly claimed it as my own. This is simply the best lemon tart everyone who's ever tasted it has ever eaten. (They've told me so.) And I admit I've always loved taking all the credit.

When I had Bonnie Fare Catering, this was the dessert — in individual tartlet form — most often requested by my clients. Ending a dinner party on this über-satisfying note made hosts and guests alike happy and content — and prompted the guests to ask for my business card.

This lemon tart has "It," the thing that all cooks strive for: Balance. It has that "just right" Goldilocks golden mean: not TOO anything. It's not too sweet, not too tart, not too thick, and not too light. And the best news is it's not too hard to make either. It's as pretty as a clear summer's day and as refreshing as a cool ocean breeze off of the Florida coast, near where lemon trees grow.

The six simple ingredients in this delicate tart are available everywhere, year-round. It's appropriate for any occasion, be it a June graduation dinner or a Christmas feast. So when you have a lemon — or two or three — make this lemon tart. It will soon become your signature dessert too. (But don't forget to credit me.)

Bonnie Fare Lemon Tart

For Pastry

Prepare 1 prebaked 9" lemony tart shell.*

Ingredients

- ⅓ cup freshly squeezed lemon juice (not bottled)
- 2 teaspoons grated lemon zest
- ¼ cup (½ stick) unsalted butter, melted and cooled slightly
- 2 large eggs
- ¼ cup sour cream (not low-fat or lite)
- ¾ cup sugar

Procedure

1. Preheat oven to 350 degrees. Whisk filling ingredients together until well blended.

2. Pour filling into baked tart shell and bake at 350 for about 15 minutes, until set. Cool on wire rack. Dust with confectioners' sugar.

---

* *If tart pastry making is new for you, please be sure to read the Pastry chapter beginning on page 67 for all of your options and the step-by-step directions.*

Recipe Lost and Found

I'd been searching for this recipe everywhere. I looked in all of my cookbooks and in all of my notebooks. I hunted online. But I came up empty-handed and discouraged. I had so much wanted to include this recipe in this *Sweet Tarts* collection.

The memory of this tart, which I'd made in New York for autumn dinner parties when I had Bonnie Fare Catering, was so vivid in my mind, the tart was so unusual, so pretty and tasty, I just *had* to find the recipe and share it in this book.

It was a red-wine tart, decorated with grape-leaf cookies and frosted champagne grapes. It was a work of art.

When I couldn't find the recipe online, I was surprised. *Isn't everything available online?* I was beginning to give up my hope of including it in this collection. Then I stumbled upon the recipe in my old recipe-notebook — misfiled under "R," instead of "T" for tarts, where I'd first looked for it. It's from *The New York Times'* Entertainment Section, Fall 1989. *What joy! I found it!* The search was over.

This is proof that taste memories don't diminish with time. And a good recipe is a treasure that mustn't be lost or forgotten.

Red-Wine Tart (or Tartlets) with Frosted Champagne Grapes

For Pastry

Prepare 1 prebaked 9" tart shell, or 4 prebaked tartlet shells.

Ingredients

- 2 cups Gallo Burgundy wine, infused with (i.e., simmered for about 5 minutes, or until flavorful, with) lemon zest, cloves, and cinnamon stick
- 2 tablespoons unsalted butter
- ⅓ cup all-purpose flour
- 3 tablespoons sugar
- Cinnamon-sugar for sprinkling over top

Procedure

1. Preheat oven to 375 degrees.

2. To make filling: Melt butter in medium saucepan, add flour and sugar, whisking.

3. Gradually add wine (strained of zest, cloves, and cinnamon stick) and cook, stirring, until sauce becomes stiff. Pour into cooked pastry shell(s) and allow to cool.

4. Sprinkle cinnamon-sugar on tart(s). Bake until pastry is golden and sugar has formed a glaze, about 25 minutes.

5. Garnish (if desired) with pastry leaves and frosted grapes. Serve with whipped cream.

---

* If tart pastry making is new for you, please be sure to read the Pastry chapter beginning on page 67 for all of your options and the step-by-step directions.

Optional: Make grape-leaf-shape cookies by using leftover pastry scraps, baked separately, and reserved for garnish.

Optional: Make frosted grapes by using 8 ounces of champagne grapes dipped in one whisked egg white, coated with sugar, and allowed to dry on parchment paper.

A Sweet Tart Education

*A*lthough I'd been cooking all my life (I'd assisted my mother in the kitchen since early childhood, and I began cooking dinner for my family at the age of eleven, when my mother returned to work full time), I'd never baked a tart — nor, I should add, learned how to make one — until I attended cooking school in 1985, at the age of forty.

This was a drastic, midlife move for me: to quit my well paying job as a writer and editor in the New York corporate world to pursue a culinary career. But I felt I *had* to do it. Cooking made me happy. I didn't have a family to cook for, so I decided I'd cook for others — and be paid for my pleasurable efforts.

First, though, I knew I needed professional training. So I signed up for the professional-intensive program at the New York Cooking School (then Peter Kump's, now the Institute of Culinary Education [ICE]) and graduated with a blue ribbon diploma six months later. Nick Malgieri, a renowned pastry chef, culinary arts instructor, and cookbook author, was just starting his career then and taught us his eager students the tricks of his trade, with humor and panache.

There *are* tricks to making tarts, I learned from Nick, which is why relatively few home cooks attempt them. Unless you're making a rustic, free-form tart (galette), you need a special, French-design tart pan, not available everywhere. The dough needs to be fitted into this vertical- and wavy-sided, removable-bottom pan with great care (*no stretching!*), otherwise the sides shrink down in baking and the filling is likely to spill over the pastry wall. Also, when the tart shell is prebaked "blind" (empty), it must be fitted with foil and weighed down (with rice or dried beans or pennies or ceramic pie weights) to keep the pastry from puffing up in the middle.

Yes, it gets pretty tricky. But, like everything else in life, once you learn how, once you get the hang of it, it's easy. And it's fun.

To spur my newfound joy in making dessert tarts, Martha Stewart's glorious cookbook *Pies & Tarts* was published by Clarkson Potter that same year. I immediately bought a copy, swooned over the photos, and attempted a number of Martha's tart recipes. My favorite among her finest offerings was the Pear-Frangipane Tart.

When I opened my own catering business in New York in 1986, I often relied on Martha Stewart's recipes because they were consistently flawless and foolproof. Her *Hors d'Oeuvres* cookbook (Clarkson Potter 1984) provided endless inspiration for cocktail party fare. And I often made her Pear-Frangipane Tart for dessert in individual tartlets for sit-down dinner parties. Martha deserved all the credit for the compliments I received.

Pear-Frangipane Tart

For Pastry
*Prepare 1 partially baked 10″ tart shell.**

Ingredients

- 6 pears poached in white wine (see poached pears recipe on page 42); poaching liquid reserved
- 1 stick (½ cup) unsalted butter, at room temperature
- ½ cup sugar
- 1 large egg
- 1 cup finely ground blanched almonds
- 3 tablespoons dark rum
- 1 teaspoon almond extract
- 1 tablespoon all-purpose flour
- ½ cup poaching liquid (see above), reduced, for glaze

Procedure

1. Preheat oven to 425 degrees. In the bowl of an electric mixer, cream the butter and sugar until light. Add the egg, almonds, rum, almond extract, and flour, and beat until smooth.

2. Spread almond mixture in tart shell. Arrange drained, thinly sliced (crosswise) pear halves on top of almond mixture, cut side down, maintaining pear shape. Bake for 45 minutes, or until tart shell is golden and the frangipane is puffed and browned.

3. Brush reduced-poaching-liquid glaze over fresh-from-the-oven tart. Serve tart at room temperature.

---

* If tart pastry making is new for you, please be sure to read the Pastry chapter beginning on page 67 for all of your options and the step-by-step directions.

Poached Pears in Puff Pastry Tartlets

*T*here's no question that I'm a big fan of purchased puff pastry sheets.

Yes, I learned how to make classic puff pastry when I was in cooking school in New York in the mid-eighties. I even recall how it's done: Envelop a slab of butter with lean dough, smack it down with a long, slim, French rolling pin, roll it to a good-size rectangle, fold it into thirds, wrap well and chill; then smack down, roll out, fold up, wrap and chill many more times over the next few hours. I know what this effort produces and why — many, many layers of flaky-thin pastry when the thin layers of butter melt away.

But, really, who wants to go to that trouble these days, when you can readily find a package of good-quality, affordable puff pastry (I like Pepperidge Farm for its dependability and availability) in the freezer section of your local food store? Making puff pastry from scratch, the old-fashioned way, the way it was done in French palace kitchens for kings and queens, may be fun to try once in your life, just to say you've done it. But if you don't have the time (*and who does?*), I say buy it.

Then follow the directions on the back of the box for thawing and unfolding.

There are countless ways you can use these sheets to make fancy-looking, golden, light, flaky, melt-in-the-mouth pastries to impress your guests. Here is one I liked to make for Bonnie Fare Catering dinner party desserts:

First, I cut out a large size (about the size of my hand) pear shape from a piece of poster board, then I used it (wrapped in aluminum foil) as a template for cutting (with a pastry cutter) identical pear shapes from the puff pastry sheets.

Then I placed a poached pear half (partially sliced lengthwise to slightly fan it out at the bottom) on each pear-shape pastry cutout, egg washed the pastry border surrounding each pear half, and baked them at 400 degrees for about 20 – 25 minutes, until the pastry became puffed and golden brown. (See photo on page 39.)

Poached Pears

Ingredients

- 1 bottle dry white wine (such as Pinot Grigio)
- ¾ cup sugar
- 10 star anise
- zest of 1 lemon
- 1 inch piece of fresh ginger, peeled and thinly sliced
- 4 firm Bosc or Bartlett pears, peeled, cored, and halved

Procedure

1. Combine the wine and flavorings in a medium saucepan and cook for about 30 minutes at a gentle simmer, uncovered.

2. Add the pear halves to this syrup and cook until the pears are tender. (The timing will depend on the ripeness of the pears.) The tip of a knife should enter easily.

3. Remove pears gently with a slotted spoon and drain. Continue cooking syrup to reduce and use as glaze on baked tartlets. (Follow instructions for assembly in text and photos on pages 40 and 41.)

Pecan Tart
La Colombe d'Or Story

One of the purest joys for me when I was in the food business
in New York in the 1980s and '90s was visiting some of
Manhattan's hottest restaurants at the time and learning from their
food. I was especially fortunate, too, to be invited to join my friend
Gail Zweigenthal from time to time when her work obliged her
to check out the restaurants her magazine was about to review.
At the time, Gail was the editor-in-chief of *Gourmet*.

My favorite of all the restaurants we visited was La Colombe d'Or
("the golden dove"), a French Provençal-style bistro in the Gramercy
Park neighborhood, inspired by the owners' favorite restaurant in the
South of France, the famed La Colombe d'Or of St.-Paul-de-Vence.
As restaurant critic Bryan Miller of the *New York Times* said in his
three-star review of New York's own La Colombe d'Or in September
1988, then-chef Wayne Nish "turns out an impressive range of dishes
that evoke the sunny and fragrant cuisine of southern France."

This small, cozy, New York bistro felt homey to me, with its terra
cotta floor, country-fabric-covered banquettes, whitewashed brick
walls, and gentle lighting. It was filled with the charms of Provence
— a region I'd visited and fallen deeply in love with the summer I
turned forty. I was transported.

It must have been one autumn when Gail and I ate at La Colombe d'Or because this harvest-time pecan tart was on the menu. As soon as I tasted it — the best pecan tart I'd ever had — I knew I had to have the recipe for my own catering business. People in the food world, I'd learned, are large hearted and generous by nature. And how could they refuse my request for the recipe, given the fact that the editor-in-chief of *Gourmet* was sitting across the table from me?

Helen Studley, who with her husband George opened La Colombe d'Or in New York in 1976, wrote a charming book about their experience titled *Life of a Restaurant* (Crown, NY, 1994). In it she graciously shares everything they'd learned to date about running a "mom and pop" restaurant in Manhattan, as well as all of the recipes for their signature dishes. This recipe is not in that book. I think you can only find it here. The best pecan tart you'll ever have.

Pecan Tart La Colombe d'Or

For Pastry
*Prepare 1 partially baked 10" tart shell.**

Ingredients

- 2 cups shelled pecans (1, 8-ounce bag)
- ¼ cup (packed) dark brown sugar
- ¼ cup (½ stick, or 4 tablespoons) unsalted butter
- 3 ounces (about ⅓ cup) B & B liqueur
- 3 large eggs
- ½ cup dark corn syrup
- ⅓ cup molasses
- 2 tablespoons melted unsalted butter
- 1 teaspoon pure vanilla

Procedure

1. Preheat oven to 325 degrees. Combine pecans with brown sugar, butter and B&B liqueur in a saucepan and cook over medium heat, stirring, until caramelized, about 10-12 minutes. Pour into partially baked tart shell and smooth out.

2. Whisk together the eggs, corn syrup, molasses, melted butter and vanilla. Pour into tart shell on top of caramelized pecans (do not over-fill; you may find you have 1–2 tablespoons left over).

3. Bake at 325 degrees for about 45-50 minutes, until set. Serve at room temperature, each slice dolloped with sweetened whipped cream.

---

* If tart pastry making is new for you, please be sure to read the Pastry chapter beginning on page 67 for all of your options and the step-by-step directions.

Raspberry Dreams Dashed

When I left Mali, West Africa, to return to the United States to live in 2001, after having spent five years in Africa, I decided to settle in Northern New Mexico. This choice wouldn't surprise any other American who had lived in Africa for years and loved it. Northern New Mexico, with its huge, overarching sky, raw, earthy topography, fathoms-deep cultural roots and slow pace, is remarkably reminiscent of parts of Africa.

My sister in Denver had first suggested I look into New Mexico when I was thrashing about in Mali wondering where in the world to go next. "You like third world countries," she wrote to me. "New Mexico is like a third world country," she quipped.

I bought a little house in Dixon, a farming community nestled in a lovely, fertile valley, about a half-hour's drive south of Taos. The house was surrounded by tall, old and gnarled apple trees, whose fragrant blossoms in the spring made me feel as if I lived on a perfumed cloud. In front of the house was an open, one-and-a-half-acre field, which I began to cultivate in increments, all by myself. I planted peach trees, a lavender field, a kitchen garden, and a raspberry patch the length of a bowling alley.

It had been a dream of mine, for as long as I could remember, to one day grow raspberries in my own back yard. So I lovingly tended these raspberry plants to make that dream come true.

In my kitchen garden, as in my kitchen, I experimented. Green peas and all sorts of beans did well, but zucchini didn't, due to squash bugs. Carrots did beautifully, but tomatoes needed a week or two more of summer sunshine than northern New Mexico could offer to ripen on the vine. The strawberries were sweet but sparse. The rhubarb, with its jutting, hairbrush-like stalks, amazed me with its growth.

It takes a few years, I learned, for raspberry bushes to bear fruit. But I was patient. I wasn't going anywhere. I bided my time, followed the rules, cut back the old stems, watered and mulched, rigged up a long, lattice canopy to protect these healthy plants from the strong summer sun and lower-Rocky Mountain elements.

And then late one summer, small, white, red-raspberries-to-be appeared on all of the bushes. I was elated. How I babied these babies! I had visions of bowls of fresh ripe raspberries for breakfast, jars of homemade red raspberry jam throughout the year, and of course raspberry-topped tarts to impress the guests I'd invite for tea.

Then came an early frost. On October 6th that year the nighttime temperature dropped to well below freezing, and all of my almost-ripe, not-yet-red raspberries froze to death. My heart broke. My raspberry dreams died. Soon after, I decided to sell my beloved little "farmette" and move up to Taos, where I wouldn't bother with a garden.

This tart, though, reminds me of that hopeful time. It's adapted from my friend Melissa Bell's favorite Raspberry-Rhubarb Pie recipe, which she found in the cookbook, *The Artful Pie*.

Raspberry-Rhubarb Tart

For Pastry

Prepare 1 partially baked 10" tart shell.

Ingredients

- ¾ cups sugar
- 2½ tablespoons flour (I use Wondra), divided
- 1/8 teaspoon salt
- 2 cups sliced (into ½" pieces) rhubarb stalks, fresh or frozen (thawed)
- 1 cup raspberries, fresh or frozen (thawed)
- 1 tablespoon unsalted butter, cut into small pieces

Procedure

1. Preheat oven to 400 degrees. Sprinkle ½ tablespoon of flour over the bottom of the partially baked, cooled tart shell and smooth with your hand (to fill up the holes from docking).

2. In a large mixing bowl, stir together the sugar, remaining flour, and salt. Toss well. Stir in the rhubarb and then gently fold in the raspberries. Spoon the filling into the tart shell and, with a spatula, evenly distribute.

3. Set the tart on a foil- or parchment-lined baking sheet and dot the top with the butter pieces. Bake until the pastry is golden brown and the fruit is bubbling, about 40-45 minutes.

---

* If tart pastry making is new for you, please be sure to read the Pastry chapter beginning on page 67 for all of your options and the step-by-step directions.

Wild Plums for Old Chums

Spindly little plum trees grew wild along the acequia ditch that ran the length of the field in front of my home in Dixon, New Mexico. This acequia was part of an ancient method of irrigation in this region, first devised by the indigenous Pueblo people and continued by the early Hispanic settlers. Ingeniously, these farmers guided the high mountain snowmelt in winding, dugout pathways down into their waiting thirsty fields, knowing that the rains in the high desert could not be relied upon to keep their crops alive. I was lucky, I was told, to have a place with a ditch; and I was even luckier, I felt, to have wild plum trees growing along that ditch's edge.

In early September 2006, my dear friend Ron Goldhammer, who had been my sous chef in New York when I had Bonnie Fare Catering and had since moved back to his hometown, Los Angeles, came to visit me in rural Dixon with his then-partner, now-husband, Glenn Tan. I don't remember what I cooked for us for lunch that day, but I do remember the dessert: a plum galette, made from the plump purple plums on my wild trees, served warm with vanilla ice cream. I'll never forget their handsome faces as they tasted this galette — their wide eyes and broad smiles. No "tame" plums could have tasted so good and been so memorable.

I'd followed a recipe I found in the August 2006 issue of *Gourmet* magazine, my favorite food magazine of all time. Unfortunately, that magazine, which had been published every month since 1941, ceased publication at the end of 2009, due, it was said, to "shifting food interests among the readership." For me, though, the recipes from *Gourmet* remain as enduring as old friendships and as ceaselessly surprising as wild plums.

Plum Galette

For Pastry

Prepare 1 galette pastry (page 71).

Ingredients

- 2 tablespoons semolina (or Wondra) flour
- 5 tablespoons granulated sugar, divided
- 5 large black, red, or purple plums (1½ pounds), halved, pitted, and cut lengthwise into 8 wedges
- 1 tablespoon confectioners' sugar
- ¾ cup crème fraîche or sour cream (optional)
- 1 tablespoon Armagnac or Cognac (optional)

Procedure

1. Preheat oven to 375 degrees. Line a large (17 x 12-inch) baking sheet with parchment paper.

2. Roll out dough on a lightly floured surface with a lightly floured rolling pin into a 13-inch round. Transfer to baking sheet.

3. Stir together the flour and 2 tablespoons granulated sugar and spread evenly over dough, leaving a 1-inch border. Arrange plums, skin sides down, in 1 layer on top of sugar mixture, then sprinkle plums with 3 tablespoons granulated sugar.

4. Fold in edge of dough to cover outer rim of plums, pleating dough as necessary.

5. Bake galette, loosely covered with a sheet of foil, 40 minutes. Remove foil and bake until fruit is tender and juices are bubbling, about 5 minutes more.

6. Transfer galette on baking sheet to a rack and immediately brush hot juices over plums using a pastry brush. Dust hot galette with confectioners' sugar (sugar will melt and help glaze galette). Cool to warm or room temperature, about 30 minutes.

7. *Optional:* While galette cools, stir together crème fraîche, Armagnac (if using), plus 3 tablespoons granulated sugar in a bowl until sugar is dissolved. Serve galette with Armagnac cream.

An Abundance
of Apricots

In the dead of summer 2012, when heat and drought were devastating over half the country and mainstay crops such as corn were withering on their stalks, sending warnings of dire ripple-effects throughout the economy, my then-new hometown, Taos, New Mexico, was enjoying the unusual blessings of rain and an overabundance of at least one crop: apricots. There are many years, I was told, when spring frosts kill the prospect of summer apricots. That year was not one.

Wherever I walked, I passed apricot trees by the side of the road that were heavily laden, dripping as if with raindrops, with fat, nearly ripe fruit. My first thought was to find the owners of these properties and give them my recipe for apricot jam. My second thought was, *Why didn't I bring my bucket on this walk?*

That summer I edited a community fundraising cookbook titled *Storied Recipes* for Taos's literary nonprofit organization, SOMOS (the Society of the Muse of the Southwest). Among that cookbook's 84 stories-with-recipes was one for Apricot-Ginger Jam. Armed with this recipe and a big blue pail, I visited a generous friend's two apricot trees and gleefully helped myself. In one compulsive week I managed to make four batches of this over-the-top-delicious jam. Then I gave the golden jars as gifts.

Apricot-Ginger Jam

For each batch of apricot jam I used 2 quarts of washed, pitted, fresh Taos apricots; 5 cups sugar; ¼ cup minced fresh ginger; the zest and juice of one lemon; ¼ teaspoon almond extract; and a half pouch of liquid pectin. I cooked all but the pectin in a large, heavy-bottom pot, stirring frequently, for 40-50 minutes, adding the pectin in the last few minutes. This recipe makes about 6 half-pint jars of what recipients exclaim is "the best jam in the world!"

Apricot-Ginger Tart

For Pastry

Prepare 1 prebaked 10″ tart shell.*

Ingredients

- 2 cups apricot-ginger jam (page 56), or good-quality store-bought apricot jam
- 1 tablespoon freshly minced (or grated), peeled ginger root (if using store-bought jam)
- 8-10 ripe apricots (preferably in season), washed, halved and pitted

Procedure

1. Preheat oven to 375 degrees. Spread jam into the cooled tart shell, evenly. Sprinkle with ginger (if using store-bought apricot jam).

2. Place apricots, cut-side down, onto the jam in one layer. Place tart on parchment-lined baking sheet and bake until fruit is cooked and jam is bubbly, about 20-25 minutes.

3. Glaze, if desired: Cook a small amount of jam (about ¼ cup) with an equal amount of water to boiling; strain. Use this strained liquid to brush over the top of the apricots to make the tart shine.

---

* *If tart pastry making is new for you, please be sure to read the Pastry chapter beginning on page 67 for all of your options and the step-by-step directions.*

Thanksgiving Offerings

One Thanksgiving, as a guest at the home of my friend Delma Barron's daughter in Taos, I was embraced by their annual tradition. Every year for many years Delma's daughter Linda invited about two dozen friends and friends-of-friends to join in her and her husband's favorite holiday celebration.

They converted their large, sun-bathed living room into an immense dining room with long, festively decorated harvest tables. Each of the guests brought a dish to the feast. The dishes were then displayed on the kitchen's enormous island as a buffet, and before anyone took a plate, the entire group circled the island with clasped hands and shared aloud in turn their reasons for being thankful.

Except for Delma, everyone at this gathering had been a stranger to me when I arrived. Being an introvert, I find such groups difficult to enter. But just the act of holding hands and listening to everyone's heartfelt thankfulness broke through the ice and isolation for me. The message my heart heard was: We all belong to the same family, the Family of Man(kind); we all have the same hungers; we're all thankful to be alive and to be here.

My contribution to this unforgettable feast was (of course!) tarts. I brought my famous Lemon Tart, an Apple Galette, and this Cranberry-Walnut Tart, which seems to me to have "Thanksgiving" written all over it.

Cranberry-Walnut Tart

For Pastry
Prepare 1 prebaked 9" tart shell.*

Ingredients
- 2 large eggs
- ½ cup (packed) dark brown sugar
- ⅓ cup honey
- ⅓ cup unsalted butter, melted and cooled
- a pinch of salt
- 1 teaspoon pure vanilla extract
- 1 cup whole fresh cranberries, picked over, washed and dried
- 1 cup walnuts

Procedure

1. Preheat oven to 350 degrees. Combine in a food processor the eggs, brown sugar, honey, melted butter, salt, and vanilla. Process until smooth. Add cranberries and walnuts and pulse just until roughly chopped.

2. Pour filling into shell and bake at 350 until set and golden, about 40-45 min.

------

* If tart pastry making is new for you, please be sure to read the Pastry chapter beginning on page 67 for all of your options and the step-by-step directions.

Variations
and Adaptations

*T*he tired old truism, "there's nothing new under the sun"
certainly applies to cooking. In this business everyone
borrows — or steals — ideas from everyone else, and it's considered
fair game. Oftentimes, too, mistakes are deliberately (mis)labeled
as "creations." Take the Tatin sisters' "flop," for instance, that became
the world-renowned Tarte Tatin. In the big mixing bowl called
Culinary Arts, there's a whole lot of flexibility, creativity, and
generosity. No one, to my knowledge, can copyright a recipe.

To me, it's all about variations and adaptations, extensions of
larger life lessons. Living in other parts of the world has certainly
taught me this. When I served in the Peace Corps in Gabon, Central
Africa, for instance, and my friend Gail Zweigenthal airmailed me
copies of *Gourmet* magazine every month, I tried to adapt whatever
Gourmet recipes I could to the local available produce. What a
formidable challenge! I documented those efforts in my book
How to Cook a Crocodile (Peace Corps Writers, 2010). Did I steal ideas
from *Gourmet?* Sure. But I was careful to give them attribution.

After returning to the States from Africa and living in northern
New Mexico, I learned more lessons in adaptation, in both life and
in cooking. Take, for example, the traditional prune pie, served at

festive events at Taos Pueblo and often offered for sale by Pueblo bakers at the Taos Farmers Market. According to food historian Fayne Lutz, the Taos Pueblo peoples have always gathered the wild plums that grow in profusion in the Taos area and dried them to use as a ready source of Vitamin C. Spanish settlers simply adapted the wild plum to use in a two-crusted pie, which has since become a regional favorite.

My variation on this theme is, of course, a tart because to me tarts trump pies. The following recipe is adapted from celebrated French chef Michel Richard's cookbook, *Home Cooking with a French Accent* (Morrow, 1993). As a tart, it's single-crusted, and it has the added crunch (and protein) of almonds. I've also given it an orange twist and substituted his Armagnac with Cointreau. Adaptation, indeed.

Orange-Infused Prune-Almond Tart

For Pastry
Prepare 1 prebaked 10" tart shell. *

Ingredients
- 40 pitted prunes, plumped in hot, strong tea**
- 1 cup slivered almonds, toasted
- 1 cup confectioners' sugar
- 2 eggs
- 1 stick (½ cup) unsalted butter, at room temperature
- 2 tablespoons Cointreau (or other orange liqueur)

Procedure
1. Preheat oven to 350 degrees. Place almonds, confectioners' sugar, eggs, butter, and Cointreau in the bowl of a food processor and process until smooth. Add 15 of the drained prunes and process again until smooth.

2. Spread filling into baked tart shell. Arrange remaining prunes decoratively on top. Bake at 350 degrees for about 50 minutes. Cool on a wire rack.

---

* *If tart pastry making is new for you, please be sure to read the Pastry chapter beginning on page 67 for all of your options and the step-by-step directions.*

** *Place prunes in a medium bowl. Add 4 Lipton Mandarin & Orange Green Tea teabags, cover with boiling water, then cover bowl with a plate, and let the prunes steep in this orange-flavored tea for at least an hour.*

A Slimmer, Trimmer Tart

In addition to teaching English and Creative Writing at the University of New Mexico branch in Taos for ten years, I also taught cooking in their Culinary Arts program. In this respect, I came full circle: my first experience teaching culinary arts was at the New York Cooking School in the late-eighties. And in both New York and Taos I taught, among other culinary courses, Healthy Cooking.

In my Healthy Cooking classes I taught techniques for making delicious food that happens to be also "good for you." Deprivation was not on our menu, because, of course, it doesn't work. Being creative — finding newer ways to make meals that are tasty, healthy, and appealing to the whole family — was our highest priority.

One example of my approach was this "pizza-style" tart, which I took from Mark Bittman of the *New York Times*. Tarts by nature are half the thickness of pies (and therefore half the calories if made from the same ingredients), but this tart is even thinner. The dough is rolled out flat like a huge cookie, the thin-thin slices of apple (or pear) are placed in one layer on top, like a flower, a little sugar and butter are drizzled on top, and when it's baked — preferably on a pizza pan — it looks just like a pizza. My students loved it, and those who were parents of young children reported that it was a hit at home.

Apple (or Pear) "Pizza" Tart

For Pastry

Prepare 1 galette pastry (page 71).

Ingredients

- 3 or 4 baking apples or pears, peeled, cored, and very thinly sliced
- 2 tablespoons brown sugar
- 1 tablespoon unsalted butter, cut into small bits

Procedure

1. Preheat oven to 400 degrees. On a lightly floured surface, roll or pat dough into a 10-inch circle. Transfer circle to a parchment-paper-lined baking sheet. Arrange fruit slices on top, right out to the edges, in an attractive pattern.

2. Sprinkle fruit slices with brown sugar and dot with butter bits. Bake until crust is nicely browned and fruit is tender, about 20-30 minutes. Cut with a pizza cutter.

On the Poetry
of Perfect Pastry

I'm not a poet, and I don't believe in human perfection. So why am I attempting to write about the poetry of perfect pastry? Because essays, as this one is, are by definition attempts to make some sense of things not well understood.

For me, as a non-poet, recipes are analogous to poetry: thoughtful, artful, concentrated guides for life. Gather these ingredients, the recipe says (or these images, the poem says), then follow these directions (or this train of thought), and *voila*, you'll create something useful, fresh, and new — food to eat (from the recipe), or food for thought (from the poem.) And, like recipes, poetry requires some *doing* — concentration, application. You've got to throw yourself into the effort to get the best results.

As for striving for perfection, I'm too much of a realist. *We're not in Heaven yet,* I often remind myself, *so don't set your sights unrealistically high.* Perfection may be out of human reach, but trying one's best is always doable and laudable. And risking failure by trying new things is part of the excitement.

I'm reminded of a poem by the 19th century American poet James Russell Lowell, "For an Autograph," which I learned in high school and which still rumbles around in my mind. It reads in part:

"...Life is a leaf of paper white
Whereon each one of us may write
His word or two, and then comes night.
...Greatly begin! Though thou have time
But for a line, be that sublime,
Not failure, but low aim, is crime."

— James Russell Lowell

Lowell, of course, was referring to writing about your life. But I'll take poetic license and extend the thought to pastry making. Yes, it's tricky, but don't let that stop you. *Greatly begin!* Aim high! Though your results, like mine, may never reach the pinnacle of perfection, they'll always be delicious and pretty.

Here are my favorite sweet pastry dough recipes. I choose certain ones for some things, like the lemony one for the lemon tart and the addition of an egg yolk to the galette dough. But one could, in fact, use the basic all-butter pastry dough recipe for all. So I'll let you choose among the ones I've gathered, tried, and liked over the years.

Keep trying! And don't be afraid to fail. We're not in Heaven yet.

Basic All-Butter Pastry

~ Makes enough for a 9" or 10" tart shell ~

Ingredients

- 1¼ cups all-purpose flour
- ¼ teaspoon salt
- 1 stick (½ cup) cold unsalted butter, cut into ½" dice*
- 3–4 tablespoons ice water

Procedure

1. In a large bowl, whisk together flour and salt. Blend in butter with your fingertips or a pastry blender (or pulse in a food processor) until mixture resembles coarse meal. Drizzle evenly with 3 tablespoons ice water and gently stir with a fork (or pulse in processor) until incorporated.

2. Squeeze a small handful; if it doesn't hold together, add more ice water, ½ tablespoon at a time, stirring (or pulsing) until just incorporated, then test again. (Do not overwork, or pastry will be tough.)

3. Turn out mixture onto a lightly floured surface and divide into four portions. With the heel of your hand, smear each portion once or twice in a forward motion to help distribute the butter. Gather dough together and press into a ball, then flatten into a 5-inch disk.

4. Refrigerate, wrapped tightly in plastic wrap, until firm, at least one hour.

---

* *Sometimes I freeze a stick of butter and grate it into the bowl of flour using the largest holes of a hand grater, instead of cutting it into ½" dice.*

Lemony Pastry for Lemon Tart

~ Makes enough for 9" tart shell ~

Ingredients

- 1 cup all-purpose flour
- 1 tablespoon sugar
- ⅛ teaspoon salt
- ½ teaspoon grated lemon zest
- 1 stick (½ cup) cold unsalted butter, cut up
- 1 teaspoon freshly squeezed lemon juice
- 1½ tablespoons (or a bit more) ice water

Procedure

Follow procedure for Basic All-Butter Pastry on page 69.

Galette, or Free-Form Tart, Sweet Pastry

~ Makes enough for a 13" circle ~

Ingredients

- 1¼ cup all-purpose flour (or 1 cup all-purpose plus ¼ cup cake flour)
- 3 tablespoons sugar
- a pinch of salt
- 1 stick unsalted butter, frozen
- 1 egg yolk
- 3–4 tablespoons ice water

Procedure

1. Sift flour, sugar and salt together into a medium bowl (or directly onto your pastry board).

2. Using the largest holes on a hand grater, grate the frozen stick of butter into the flour mixture, tossing with your hand from time to time to distribute the butter evenly. Pinch the flour-butter mixture with your fingertips (i.e., the coolest part of your hands) to combine well.

3. In a small bowl, whisk together the egg yolk and ice water and pour into the center of the flour-butter mixture.

4. Working quickly with your fingertips, form into a dough and pat the dough into a disk. Wrap disk with plastic wrap and refrigerate until cold and firm, about one hour.

BB's Pâte Sucrée

My variation on the French classic
~ Makes enough for a 10" tart shell ~

Ingredients

- 1 cup all-purpose flour
- ¼ cup cake flour
- ¼ teaspoon salt
- ¼ cup confectioners' sugar
- 1 stick (½ cup) unsalted butter, frozen
- ¼ cup ice-cold water

Procedure

1. In a medium bowl combine the two flours, salt, and confectioners' sugar; whisk well.

2. Using a hand-grater, grate the stick of butter on the largest holes, into the flour mixture. Toss well to distribute. Pinch the flour-butter mixture with your fingertips to combine.

3. Make a well in the center of the flour-butter mixture and add the ice water. Working quickly with your fingertips, form the dough into a disk, wrap with plastic wrap and refrigerate until cold and firm, about one hour.

Nick Malgieri's Sweet Tart Pastry

~ Makes enough for an 11" or 12" tart ~

Ingredients

- 1½ cups all-purpose flour
- ¼ cup sugar
- 1 teaspoon baking powder
- ½ teaspoon salt
- 6 tablespoons (¾ stick) cold unsalted butter, cut into 8 pieces
- 1 large egg
- 1 large egg yolk
- 1 tablespoon water

Procedure

1. Combine the flour, sugar, baking powder, and salt in the bowl of a food processor fitted with the metal blade. Pulse several times to mix.

2. Add the butter and pulse repeatedly until it is finely mixed into the dry ingredients.

3. Add the egg, egg yolk, and water. Pulse repeatedly until the dough forms a ball.

4. Turn the dough out onto a floured board. Form dough into a disk about ½-inch thick. Wrap in plastic and refrigerate until ready to use (at least one hour).

Rolling, Fitting, & Prebaking the Tart Shell

1. Once your disk of dough is cold and firm, you're ready to roll it out: Dust a work surface with flour, and, beginning in the middle of the dough, roll with even pressure to the edge. Turn (rotate) the dough (to keep it from sticking in place) and repeat this process again and again, until  the dough is several inches larger than your tart pan, between ¼ inch and 1/8 inch thick.

2. Butter the bottom and sides of your tart pan. Fold the dough into fourths and place it gently into the tart pan, pointy edge at the middle. Gently unfold the dough and loosely (as though the dough were fabric) drape it into the corners of the pan. (Do not stretch it, or the pastry will shrink up on you when baking.) With your thumb, press the dough against the wavy sides of the pan, and allow the excess dough to fall over the outside of the pan.

3. Roll your rolling pin over the top of the tart to cut off the excess dough that is falling over the edges. (Save the scraps to make pastry leaves or sugar cookies.)

4. Butter one side of a piece of aluminum foil the size of your tart. Gently place the foil, buttered side down, into the tart shell and fill it with pie weights (dried beans, rice, pennies, or ceramic pie-weight-beads).

5. Place tart pan on a baking sheet and bake the shell in a preheated 400-degree oven for about 10-15 minutes. Remove the tart shell from the oven, gently lift off the foil and pie weights, and return the tart shell to the oven to fully bake 5-10 minutes more, until the pastry is slightly golden and dry to the touch (like a cookie).

NOTE: For a partially baked tart shell, do not return to the oven to fully bake.

6. Cool tart shell (in tart pan) on a wire rack. Shell can be prebaked (or partially baked) the day before and stored at room temperature, loosely wrapped.

Removing Finished Baked Tart from Its Pan

One of the true beauties of tarts is that, unlike pies, tarts can stand alone, unsupported by their pan. Once your tart is baked and has cooled on a rack, you can carefully remove the outer ring (by holding the center-bottom with one hand and letting the outer ring drop down, or by resting the tart on a small bowl and letting the ring drop) before placing your tart regally on a fancy plate. The pastry's vertical side wall will hold the filling intact.

Postscript: Nut Crusts

There is, of course, another way to make tart crusts, which may be welcome news for pastryphobes. With this easier method, you simply press a crumbly mixture into the tart pan and up the sides. The following two recipes use this method, employing ground almonds and macadamias.

And there is another reason I've chosen these recipes. When I told my Taos friends Cherie Burns and Becky Lenzini about this "Sweet Tarts" project, Cherie asked, "Will you include a coconut tart? My husband loves all things coconut." And Becky chimed in, "What about a chocolate tart? I LOVE chocolate!"

So here you are, my Sweethearts, more tarts for you:

Coconut Cream Tart with Macadamia Nut Crust

~ Makes one 11" tart ~

Ingredients

For crust:

- 1⅓ cups salted macadamia nuts (about 7 ounces)
- 1 stick (½ cup) cold unsalted butter, cut into pieces
- 1½ cups all-purpose flour
- ¼ cup sugar
- 2 large egg yolks

For filling:

- 1½ teaspoons unflavored gelatin
- 2 tablespoons dark rum
- 8 large egg yolks
- ½ cup plus 2 tablespoons sugar
- 2 cups well-stirred canned unsweetened coconut milk
- 1 cup well-chilled heavy cream
- ¾ cup sweetened flaked coconut

Procedure

1. Preheat oven to 350 degrees. In a baking pan toast nuts in one layer in middle of oven until golden, about 10 minutes (watch closely); cool. Finely chop ⅔ cup nuts. Coarsely chop remaining ⅔ cup nuts and reserve.

2. In a bowl with a pastry blender or in a food processor, blend or pulse together finely chopped nuts, flour, sugar, and butter until mixture resembles coarse meal. Add yolks and blend dough until

78

it begins to come together but is still crumbly. Press dough in bottom and up sides of an 11" tart pan with a removable bottom. Chill 30 minutes.

3. Preheat oven to 375 degrees. Bake crust in middle of oven until golden, about 25 minutes, and transfer to a rack to cool completely.

4. To make the filling: In a small bowl, sprinkle gelatin over rum to soften 5 minutes. In another bowl, whisk together yolks, sugar, and a pinch of salt.

5. In a large saucepan, bring coconut milk to a boil and remove pan from heat. Gradually whisk half of coconut milk into yolk mixture and whisk back into pan with remaining coconut milk. Cook custard over moderate heat, whisking constantly, until thickened and a thermometer registers 170 degrees, about 12 minutes. (Do not let custard boil.)

6. Remove pan from heat and add gelatin mixture, whisking until gelatin is dissolved. Transfer custard to a bowl to cool and chill, stirring frequently, until thickened but not set, about 30 minutes.

7. Beat cream to soft peaks and fold into custard. Pour filling into crust. Chill about 4 hours. Remove rim and sprinkle top with coconut and reserved nuts.

Chocolate Ganache Tart with Almond Crust

~ Makes one 9" tart ~

Ingredients

For crust:

- 1⅓ cups sliced almonds
- ½ cup sugar
- 3 tablespoons unsalted butter, melted

For filling:

- 12 ounces good-quality bittersweet or semi-sweet chocolate, chopped
- 1 cup heavy cream
- ⅓ cup sour cream
- ⅓ cup sugar
- 1 egg yolk
- ¼ cup sliced almonds

Procedure

1. Preheat oven to 350 degrees. Place sliced almonds and sugar in the bowl of a food processor and process until finely chopped. Add melted butter and process until mixture comes together.

2. Press nut mixture into bottom and up sides of a 9" tart pan with a removable bottom. Bake until golden brown, about 15 minutes. Cool on a rack.

3. To make the filling: Place chocolate in a large, microwaveable bowl. Heat in microwave oven for 1½ minutes on High. Stir. Heat for another 1½ minutes. Stir until smooth.

4. In a medium saucepan add heavy cream, sour cream, sugar and egg yolk. Cook over medium heat, whisking constantly, until bubbles form around edges. (Do not boil.) Gradually add to melted chocolate and stir until smooth.

5. Pour ganache into cooled crust, smoothing the surface, and sprinkle sliced almonds around the edges. Chill tart before serving.

Recipe Index

Measurement Conversion Tables

Volume Conversions:

US Customary Quantity	Metric Equivalent
1 teaspoon	5 mL
1 tablespoon	15 mL
2 tablespoons	30 mL
1/4 cup or 2 fluid ounces	60 mL
1/3 cup	80 mL
1/2 cup or 4 fluid ounces	120 mL
2/3 cup	160 mL
3/4 cup or 6 fluid ounces	180 mL
1 cup or 8 fluid ounces or 1/2 pint	240 mL
1 ½ cup or 12 fluid ounces	360 mL
2 cups or 1 pint or 16 fluid ounces	500 mL
3 cups or 1 ½ pints	700 mL
4 cups or 2 pints or 1 quart	950 mL
4 quarts or 1 gallon	3.8 L
1 ounce	28 grams
1/4 lb. (4 ounces)	112 grams
1/2 lb. (8 ounces)	225 grams
3/4 lb. (12 ounces)	337 grams
1 lb. (16 ounces)	450 grams

Note: When a high level of precision is not required, basic equivalents may be used as follows:

1 cup = 250 mL

1 pint = 500 mL

1 quart = 1 L

1 gallon = 4 L

Weight Conversions:

US Customary Quantity	Metric Equivalent
1 ounce	28 grams
4 ounces or ½ pound	113 grams
⅓ pound	150 grams
8 ounces or ½ pound	230 grams
⅔ pound	300 grams
12 ounces or ¾ pound	340 grams
16 ounces or 1 pound	450 grams
32 ounces or 2 pounds	900 grams

Note: The ounces referred to in this weight conversion table are not fluid ounces.

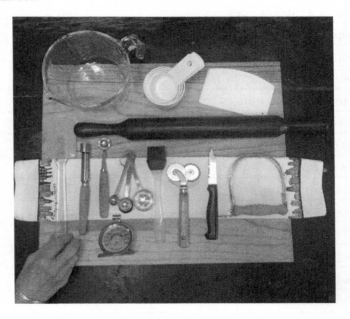

Acknowledgements

Many sweethearts deserve acknowledgement and thanks for helping to inspire this collection of stories and recipes: My baking guru, renowned cooking instructor and cookbook author Nick Malgieri, for first teaching me how to make French tarts; my friend, former editor-in-chief at *Gourmet*, Gail Zweigenthal, for inviting me to La Colombe D'Or; my culinary comrade and fellow-New York caterer, Carol Durst-Wertheim, for lasting friendship; beloved members of my former staff at Bonnie Fare Catering with whom I'm still in close touch — Ron Goldhammer, Michael Marotta, Paul Matteo, and John North; and the special women who came to my tea-and-tart tastings in Taos, New Mexico, when I lived there and while I was writing these true stories — Cherie Burns, Lorraine Ciancio, Teresa Dovalpage, Judith Kendall, Rebecca Lenzini, Barbara Scott, Jan Smith, and Pamela Wagner.

I shared this collection with those sweethearts in photocopied form then, but now that it's grown into a published book, I have more special sweethearts to thank for making this happen: *mis amigos* (and tart tasters) here in San Miguel de Allende, Mexico — Cynthia Claus, Catherine Marenghi, Sy Zachar and Bill Gerich; old friends Beatriz and Dan Villegas, and Maria Edith Rodriguez Matehuala; my talented new friend and enthusiastic tart-baking student, Kharin Gilbert, who photographed most of my fresh-baked tarts for it; Kathy Munroe of Starr Design, who designed this book's interior, as well as its cover (and two of my previous books' covers);

and my granddaughter-in-law, Julie C. Loughlin, who staged the photo of her sweet-sweet twin daughters, my great-granddaughters, to whom this book is dedicated.

About Bonnie

*F*or Bonnie, writing and cooking have always been analogous. Both involve the thoughtful, careful, and, ideally, loving preparation of something good for another's consumption. Both are determined efforts to convey something nourishing — one to the body, the other to the mind and soul — to someone outside of oneself.

Bonnie has been travelling these parallel tracks for most of her professional life. She is the author of many published essays, as well as four published books: most recently, the historical novel *Jamie's Muse* (Nighthawk Press, 2018), based on the lives of her Scottish great-grandparents who emigrated to South Africa in the late 19th century; and three memoirs about her own life-changing experiences in various countries in Africa.

Bonnie giving a reading from Jamie's Muse *at the San Miguel Literary Sala in 2018*

Bonnie taught English and Creative Writing at the University of New Mexico's Taos branch for ten years. Now retired and living in San Miguel de Allende, Mexico, she writes a weekly blog called The WOW Factor: Words of Wisdom from Wise Older Women, which is read by hundreds of (mostly) women all over the world (www.bonnieleeblack.com/blog/).

When she had her catering business, Bonnie Fare Catering, in New York City, from 1986 to 1996, Bonnie's freelance writing focused on food. She was the cookbook reviewer for the James Beard Foundation's monthly newsletter. She also taught French cooking and Spa Cuisine at Peter Kump's New York Cooking School (now the Institute of Culinary Education [ICE]) in Manhattan for many years.

In 1996, at the age of fifty-one, Bonnie joined the U.S. Peace Corps and served for two years as a health and nutrition volunteer in the rainforest of Gabon, Central Africa, where she taught simple, sustainable, healthy cooking and revised the Peace Corps-Gabon volunteers' cookbook, *The Gabon Gourmet.*

Back in the States, she ultimately settled (for a time) in Taos, New Mexico, where she was a food columnist for *The Taos News*; the editor of *Storied Recipes,* a fundraising literary-themed cookbook for Taos's literary nonprofit, SOMOS; and a cooking instructor in UNM-Taos's Culinary Arts Department. She is featured in the book, *The Remarkable Women of Taos*, compiled and edited by the late Elizabeth Cunningham.

Bonnie is an honors graduate of the writing program at Columbia University in New York (1979), and she later earned an MFA in Creative Writing from Antioch University in Los Angeles. She studied cooking at La Varenne Ecole de Cuisine in Paris (1985) and holds a blue-ribbon diploma from Peter Kump's New York Cooking School.

For more information, visit: www.bonnieleeblack.com.

Bonnie's Other Books

Jamie's Muse
(Nighthawk Press, 2018)

The lost history of Bonnie Lee Black's Scottish great-grandmother, Helen, has haunted the author for years. Why, as young newlyweds, did Helen and William Black leave their hometown of Kirriemuir in Angus, Scotland, and emigrate to the "dark continent" of Africa in 1882?

Bonnie's deep spiritual connection to her ancestor inspired her to weave a tale, in this, her first novel, that is part imagination and part history.

Helen and Will died just three years after settling in Natal, South Africa, just months after the birth of their first child, Bonnie's grandfather, John. There is no record of their deaths; no record of how their son ended up in an orphanage in Edinburgh, nor of how the 14-year-old boy stowed away on a ship to New York.

Bonnie lived in Africa for many years herself and writes with a sure sense of place and history, interwoven with the fantasy of Helen, her short life, and her imagined close friendship with Kirriemuir's most famous son, J.M. Barrie, author of *Peter Pan*.

How To Make An African Quilt:
The Story of the Patchwork Project of Ségou, Mali
(Nighthawk Press, 2013)

How do we sew together the hoped-for future and the unfortunate past, the bright as well as the darker patches of our lives? How do we stitch cultural differences, join disparate worlds, to create something both beautiful and useful? Bonnie Lee Black subtly addresses these universal questions through vivid stories of her life-changing experience living and working in the fabled city of Ségou, Mali, West Africa, after having served for two years in the Peace Corps in Gabon.

At the request of a talented group of Malian seamstresses, Bonnie taught them the craft of American patchwork quilting and spearheaded an independent economic-development effort she called the Patchwork Project. In this memoir she has created a many-layered patchwork quilt of a book that brings that time and place — and all its colorful characters — to life on the page.

Threaded throughout is the fictional narrative of Jeneba, a slave-quilter in the antebellum American South who had been kidnapped from the Kingdom of Ségou as a child, as well as the real voices of the Malian women who took part in Ségou's Patchwork Project.

How To Cook A Crocodile:
A Memoir with Recipes
(Peace Corps Writers, 2010)

Casting caution to the wind at the age of fifty, New York caterer and food writer Bonnie Lee Black decided to close her catering business and join the Peace Corps. Posted to the tiny town of Lastoursville in the thickly rainforested interior of Gabon, Central Africa, Bonnie taught health, nutrition, and cooking — in French — primarily to local African women and children.

In the two years she served in Gabon, Bonnie developed her own healthy recipe for a purposeful life, made in equal measures of good food, safe shelter, meaningful work, and unexpected love. Like M.F.K. Fisher's classic World War II-era book, *How to Cook a Wolf,* Bonnie's true stories comprise a lively, literary, present-day survival guide.

How to Cook a Crocodile won first prize in the "Charity and Community — North America" category at the Gourmand International awards ceremony held at the Folies Bergeres in Paris on March 6, 2012.

Somewhere Child
(Viking Press, 1981)

Somewhere Child is Bonnie Lee Black's astonishing memoir of how she lived through the ordeal of parental kidnapping not once, but twice — first in her suburban New Jersey community and then, several years later, in Salisbury, Rhodesia, where she had tracked her ex-husband down, and where, after a long and sensational legal battle, she once more won custody of her daughter, only to lose her yet again.

Bonnie assembled fragments of letters, journals, and court transcripts to create a spellbinding interior narrative recapturing those years. This beautifully told memoir is a compelling brief against child snatching, that perverse and tortuous form of domestic violence.

Somewhere Child is filled with love and fury and heart-wrenching pain, and is ultimately a testimony to the resilience and fierceness of the human spirit.

~ ~ ~

Note: All of Bonnie's books are available from Amazon.com.

Notes

Made in the USA
Monee, IL
12 October 2020

44829037R00062

Made in the USA
San Bernardino, CA
15 November 2017